Teacher Messages for Home

Grades K-2

Written by Katherine L. Ruggieri, M.Ed.

Illustrated by Megan Jeffries

Fearon Teacher Aids
A Division of Frank Schaffer Publications, Inc.

Editors: Kristin Eclov, Michael Batty

Cover Design: Rita Hudson

Book Design: Rose Sheifer

Art Direction: Rita Hudson

Graphic Artist: Anthony Strasburger

FE111031

Table of Contents

Introduction

About This Book

Communication between teacher and parent is the cornerstone of a successful school experience. You, the teacher, are the link between home and school. Parents need to hear from you if their children's classwork is not meeting standards, if their children's behavior is problematic, if an assignment is incomplete, if a field trip is coming up, if more supplies are needed, if their children are hurt, sick, or upset, if . . . if . . . if. . . . Keeping parents informed is often a formidable task. However, as the teacher, it is up to you to make sure that each parent is kept adequately apprised of his or her child's progress. Without a selection of pre-prepared forms, you could easily find yourself struggling to compose several notes simultaneously from scratch. An incomplete or unclear message sent home could result in confusion and additional work.

The degree of clear and open communication established with parents will have a direct and profound impact on the success and effectiveness of your school year. The forms in this book will let you get your messages to parents without having to spend time preparing a new form for every occasion. By providing forms that cover most situations, *Teacher Messages for Home* helps make that vital communication between home and school more efficient and more convenient for the teacher.

5

How to Use This Book

Each form in this book can be photocopied in advance and stored in labeled files. This way, the forms will be ready to be pulled out as needed. The use of each form will determine whether it will be needed for individual students (I) or for the whole class (WC), which will give you an idea of how many copies should be kept on hand.

The information needed for the forms can be handwritten or typed in. In some situations, a teacher may want to use a form as a guideline to create a handwritten form for a specific purpose.

To avoid confusion, the term *parent* also refers to legal guardian. In some instances, you may want to substitute the words *legal guardian* for *parent* before sending a form home.

When to Use This Book

At the beginning of the school year you will find it necessary to communicate with parents regarding many things. This is when you will establish your own communication style and the parents will form expectations for the future.

Each chapter of *Teacher Messages for Home* contains forms relating to particular needs. The table of contents lists the titles of every form in each chapter. Take the time to thumb through the book to familiarize yourself with the forms. Afterward, you will know when each is appropriate to use.

At the end of the school year, you will reflect on how often you had to send notes to parents and will realize the size of the task. The ready-made forms in *Teacher Messages for Home* will help you achieve and maintain effective communication with parents.

1. Beginning of the Year

Positive, year-long communication between teacher and parents will create the firm foundation that students need to get the most from their school experiences. As the academic year begins, a lot of important information must be sent to parents. This information, presented in a clear and timely manner, will set the expectation for productive communication throughout the year.

Welcome to the _____ Grade

This form presents the daily schedule and lists the general topics to be covered during the year. The list of topics provides an overview of general themes or subjects to be studied; the daily schedule does the same for the students' school day. Items of interest generally include activities that require students to move from one place to another, such as recess, lunch, physical education, or special activities. (WC)

Supply List for _____ Grade

This list provides a way to request basic supplies needed for the year. Be sure to describe specific needs, such as rulers that must be plastic or pencils that must have #2 lead. List supplies in two columns, one for items on which the student's name must be written, and the other for items that do not need a label. (WC)

Classroom Rules

The classroom rules sheet lists desirable qualities for classroom conduct. These rules may be modified later by you and your class, or may be considered a finished product. Copy these lists on 8-1/2" x 11" pages for posting around the classroom or enlarge them onto poster board. (WC)

Student Information

This form lists emergency information and information about the individual child. The interest items will help you get to know your students a little better and often provide ideas for individual projects or assignments. This information can be kept in your classroom, either in individual files or in one folder labeled *Current Student Information*. (WC)

Hopes and Dreams

This form is designed to let parents tell you about their children. As the teacher, it is important for you to be aware of each child's uniqueness. Parents usually welcome the opportunity to share what they believe is special about their children. Requesting this information lets parents know that you are on the same team. Keep this information on file and refer to it throughout the year. (WC)

Classroom Helpers

This form is designed to encourage parents to participate however they can. Parent helpers can be a great resource. You may want to wait until you have established your classroom expectations before inviting parents in. Send this form out when you are ready to have them help you. (WC)

Name _____

Welcome to the ____ Grade

Topics about which we will be learning:

_____

_____

_____

_____

Here is our daily schedule:

Time   **Subject**

_____ to _____ , _____

_____ to _____ , _____

_____ to _____ , _____

_____ to _____ , _____

_____ to _____ , _____

_____ to _____ , _____

Name _____

Supply List for ____ Grade

Dear Parent,

We will have a busy year full of learning. Below is a list of the things your child will need. Some items should be clearly marked with your child's name, but others need not be marked. Please send these articles to school as soon as possible.

Thanks, _____

Labeled items

_____

_____

_____

_____

_____

_____

Unlabeled

_____

_____

_____

_____

_____

_____

 Name _____

Classroom Rules

Ears listening

Eyes watching

Hands to yourself

Feet on the floor

☺ In Our Class ☺

Be a helper.

Listen.

Be kind.

Work quietly.

Student Information

Please help me get to know your child better.

Name: _____ Nickname (if any): _____

Address: _____

_____

Birthday: _____

Family members at home: _____

Favorite food: _____ Favorite hobby: _____

Favorite thing to do as a family: _____

Does your child watch television daily? _____ How much? _____

Favorite television program: _____

Does your child read daily? _____ How much? _____

Favorite type of reading: _____

Does your child have any allergies? _____

Does your child have any special restrictions or limitations? _____

_____

Please add any other information that you think would be helpful. _____

_____

Hopes and Dreams

Date: _____

Dear Parents:

It is very important for me to know your hopes and dreams for your child this year.
I know what a treasure your children are to you.

Please tell me the special things you see in _____
that you would like me to see, too. (Please attach another sheet of paper if necessary.)

_____

_____

_____

_____

_____

_____

_____

_____

_____

_____

_____

_____

Please return this form as soon as possible.
Thank you,

_____

Classroom Helpers

Classroom helpers are an important part of our classroom. Helpers can participate in many ways, such as preparing materials, working with students individually or in small groups, correcting papers, and accompanying us on field trips.

If you are interested in being a classroom helper, please complete the following form and return it to school with your child.

☐ I would like to be a weekly helper.

Best day of the week: _____ Best time of the day: _____

Area(s) in which I would like to help: _____

Special talents I have: _____

☐ I would like to be a monthly helper.

Best day of the month: _____ Best time of the day: _____

Area(s) in which I would like to help: _____

Special talents I have: _____

☐ I would like to help on field trips.   ☐ I would like to help with class parties.

☐ I would like to help by doing work at home and returning it to school with my child.

Area(s) in which I would like to help: _____

Special talents I have: _____

Signature: _____

Telephone number and best time to call: _____

2. Homework and Study Habits

Homework is an important part of the school experience, and parents, teachers, and students need to work together to ensure that it gets done. The forms in this section help parents understand what is required of their children and how their children are performing. Because young students sometimes forget why they have taken an assignment home and don't remember when it is due, these forms keep students and parents informed. Some forms require a parent signature.

Homework Calendar

This calendar provides a clear and simple way for students to keep track of homework assignments and accomplishments for the entire week. Each day, assignments are written on the forms and students take them home for their parents to see. Parents sign the forms and send them back to school. This procedure is repeated each day of the week. A reward system can be used for students who get parent signatures each day of the week. (WC)

My Weekly Homework Report

This form allows quick feedback on a daily basis. It is intended to be sent home at the end of each day after the teacher has looked over the day's homework. If work needs to be redone, it can be stapled to the report. Checkmarks can be used to indicate that the homework is finished and correct. A percentage could be written to evaluate the student's homework performance. (WC)

Oops! I Forgot!

This is just a quick reminder to be used for forgotten schoolwork or other items. Copy onto brightly colored paper to make it more noticeable. (WC)

Work Slip

This can be attached to work that was not finished in class and that needs to be taken home. It tells the parents exactly what should be done and when it should be returned to school. (WC)

My Daily Report

This form is a daily behavior record. Acknowledgment of good behavior can help students working to modify their behavior. It informs parents in a nonthreatening way how their child is doing on a daily basis. These forms can be returned to school to be filed or left at home with the parents. If the form is to be left at home, make a copy. (WC)

Sorry You're Sick

Use this to tell students what assignments they have missed while sick. It can be sent home daily with work so that the student doesn't get too far behind. If work is not picked up daily, list the assignments on the slips. That way, you won't have to search for what was done on each day of a child's absence. (WC)

Name _____

 # Homework Calendar

Week of _____

Monday assignment: _____

_____

Parent signature: _____

Tuesday assignment: _____

_____

Parent signature: _____

Wednesday assignment: _____

_____

Parent signature: _____

Thursday assignment: _____

_____

Parent signature: _____

Friday assignment: _____

_____

Parent signature: _____

Name _____

My Weekly Homework Report

Teacher: _____

Week of _____ Room: _____

MONDAY

Homework turned in: ☐ YES ☐ NO

Homework completely finished: ☐ YES ☐ NO

Homework correct: ☐ YES ☐ NO

Try again: ☐ YES ☐ NO

TUESDAY

Homework turned in: ☐ YES ☐ NO

Homework completely finished: ☐ YES ☐ NO

Homework correct: ☐ YES ☐ NO

Try again: ☐ YES ☐ NO

WEDNESDAY

Homework turned in: ☐ YES ☐ NO

Homework completely finished: ☐ YES ☐ NO

Homework correct: ☐ YES ☐ NO

Try again: ☐ YES ☐ NO

THURSDAY

Homework turned in: ☐ YES ☐ NO

Homework completely finished: ☐ YES ☐ NO

Homework correct: ☐ YES ☐ NO

Try again: ☐ YES ☐ NO

FRIDAY

Homework turned in: ☐ YES ☐ NO

Homework completely finished: ☐ YES ☐ NO

Homework correct: ☐ YES ☐ NO

Try again: ☐ YES ☐ NO

 **Oops! I Forgot!**

Date: _____

Your child, _____ ,

forgot to bring his/her _____

to school today.

Please help him/her to remember to bring it tomorrow.

Thank you,

_____

✂ — ✂

Oops! I Forgot!

Date: _____

Your child, _____ ,

forgot to bring his/her _____

to school today.

Please help him/her to remember to bring it tomorrow.

Thank you,

_____

Work Slip

Date: _____

Your child, _____ ,

needs to work on his/her _____

and return it to school tomorrow.

Signed,

_____

 # Work Slip

Date: _____

Your child, _____ ,

needs to work on his/her _____

and return it to school tomorrow.

Signed,

_____

Name _____

My Daily Report

Week of _____

| **Monday** | I was a good listener. | I finished my work. | I got along with others. |

| **Tuesday** | I was a good listener. | I finished my work. | I got along with others. |

| **Wednesday** | I was a good listener. | I finished my work. | I got along with others. |

| **Thursday** | I was a good listener. | I finished my work. | I got along with others. |

| **Friday** | I was a good listener. | I finished my work. | I got along with others. |

Sorry you're sick. Please get well soon. We miss you!

Work for _____ Date: _____

Writing _____

Math _____

Reading _____

Spelling _____

Social studies/science _____

Special information _____

- - - ✂ - ✂ - - -

Sorry you're sick. Please get well soon. We miss you!

Work for _____ Date: _____

Writing _____

Math _____

Reading _____

Spelling _____

Social studies/science _____

Special information _____

3. Organizational Tools and Calendars

A student whose work habits are well organized has a good chance of having a productive and satisfactory school experience. The basic tools of organization can be taught to students at any age. Knowing these enables both the child and his or her parents to keep track of the numerous activities of a school day.

Monthly Calendar

This calendar template serves a twofold purpose: it can be used for practice filling in months and dates or for scheduling assignments. Tell the students which activities or assignments go on which dates, and they can complete the calendar in class. The calendar can include assignment due dates, field trips, long-term projects, and other items. (WC)

What Did I Do Today?

This form addresses the age-old question that parents like to ask and students seldom know how to answer: "What did you do today?" Space is provided for students to make daily notes of three or four things they did in school on each day of the week. Entries might include *math—adding, science—magnets, language—nouns, and art—paint*. Check the students' papers before they leave. A smiley face or star can indicate that you have seen the paper and consider it ready to go home. A weekly reward will encourage students to keep track of their papers and to take them home and bring them back to school each day. (WC)

My Weekly Goal

This is a basic goal sheet for students to complete at school and take home for parents to review. It can be completed on Monday as a class activity. Write suggestions on the board for students to copy onto their goal sheets. Goals should be as specific as possible and written in child-friendly language. Goals might include the following: *get my work finished, write my spelling words 5 times every night, read for 15 minutes each night*, and *make my Rs the right way*. (WC)

Classroom News

This template gives you an opportunity to communicate with the parents about what has happened in the classroom during a given week. The form can be filled out daily or at the end of the week and sent home with students on Fridays. Notes can be added to remind parents about upcoming events or assignments or to thank them for help on field trips or class activities. Weekly communication helps parents feel involved and informed. When you use this form, consistency is important. Parents will become accustomed to seeing it on Fridays. (WC)

Name _____

Monthly Calendar

Calendar for the month of

Sunday	Monday	Tuesday	Wednesday	Thursday	Friday	Saturday

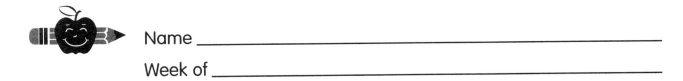

Name _____

Week of _____

What Did I Do Today?

Monday _____

_____

Parent signature: _____

Tuesday _____

_____

Parent signature: _____

Wednesday _____

_____

Parent signature: _____

Thursday _____

_____

Parent signature: _____

Friday _____

_____

Parent signature: _____

 Name _____

Date: _____

Dear _____ ,

This week in school my goal is
_____

_____

_____

_____

_____

_____

_____ .

Please help me accomplish my goal. Thank you.

Signed, _____

# Classroom News

Week of _____

Teacher: _____ Room: _____

Monday	Tuesday
Wednesday	**Thursday**
Friday	**Notes**

4. School Events

During the school year there will be many opportunities for parents to be involved in school activities. For children, sharing their school, their classroom, and their work with their parents can be a positive experience. Let parents know about school activities or events as far in advance as you can.

Event Calendar

This calendar provides space to highlight events during a given month and gives parents the chance to plan ahead. Write the time each activity begins and ends so parents know how much time is involved. (WC)

Join Us!

This is an invitation to parents to come to the classroom for a special event, such as a presentation of reports, an art activity, a play or skit, or a special guest speaker. Let parents know exactly when the event will start and how long it will last so they can make the necessary arrangements. (WC)

Open House

This invitation tells parents that you are looking forward to seeing them in your classroom. It lets them know when your classroom will be open and what will be featured in your room. (WC)

Helpers Needed

Many events require parent help. This request lets parents know what is planned and what type of help is needed. (WC)

Thank You

Thank-you notes are an important part of your communication with parents. The notes let parents know how much you appreciate them. Students can add handwritten notes. (WC)

Name _____

Event Calendar

For the month of _____

Sunday	Monday	Tuesday	Wednesday	Thursday	Friday	Saturday

reproducible

Join Us!

Please come to our classroom on _____ .

We will be

_____

_____

_____ .

Please join us from _____ to _____ .

Hope to see you there!

Open House

Date: _____

Please come visit our classroom and see what's new.

Our room, _____, will be open from _____ to _____ .

We have been working hard and want to show you our

_____

_____

_____ .

Please
join us.

Helpers Needed

Our school is having a _____

on _____ .

We're doing this to _____

_____ .

We would like to have help.

We need people to _____

_____ .

Please let me know if you would like to help.

Thank you.

Signed,

_____

Thank You!

Dear _____ ,

Thank you for helping out!
We couldn't have done it without you!

From all of us in Room _____

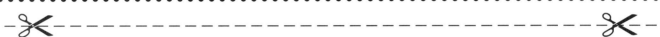

Thank You!

Dear _____ ,

Thank you for helping out!
We couldn't have done it without you!

From all of us in Room _____

reproducible

5. Field Trips

Field trips can be a great part of the school experience. They offer opportunities to take learning beyond the school site. Field trips must be thoroughly planned well in advance to be sure that things go smoothly. As soon as your field trip is scheduled, let parents know.

Field Trip Announcement

This informs parents about upcoming field trips. It lets them know when, where, and why. Space is provided on the same form to let parents know if they are needed to help. (WC)

Field Trip Reminder

This reminds parents and students about the upcoming field trip. It reminds them when it is, where they will be going, and what their children need to bring. Send this out two or three days before the field trip. (WC)

Field Trip Volunteers

This form lets you inform parents whether or not you need them to help. Often you will have too many volunteers and will want to let some of them know that they are not needed this time. (WC)

Field Trip Helpers

Once parent helpers have been chosen, this form can be used to give them more specific instructions and the names of the children they will be supervising. Instructions can be tailored to fit each field trip. Parents should keep these forms with them during the trip. (WC)

Thank You

After the trip, be sure to let parents know how much you appreciate their help by sending a thank-you note. Everyone likes to feel appreciated. Students can add handwritten notes. (WC)

Field Trip Announcement

Dear Parent,

Our class will be going on a field trip on _____ .

We will go to _____

_____ .

We are going in order to _____

_____ .

We will go by _____ and will leave from _____

at _____ .

We will go back to _____ at _____ .

Parent Helpers

☐ Adult helpers are needed. Please send a note if you would like to help.

☐ Adult helpers are not needed at this time.

Supervision will be provided by_____ .

Thank you.

Signed,

_____

Field Trip Reminder

The big day
is coming!

On _____ we will go to _____ .

We are leaving from _____ at _____ .

Don't forget to bring the following:

_____

_____

_____

We're in for a great time!
Please be prompt!

Field Trip Volunteers

Dear Parent,

Thank you for volunteering to help on our field trip to _____

on_____.

☐ We have plenty of help this time. May we call if someone cancels?

☐ We need help supervising a group of children. Please arrive at school by _____.

Thanks for your support.

- - - ✂ - ✂ - - -

Field Trip Volunteers

Dear Parent,

Thank you for volunteering to help on our field trip to _____

on_____.

☐ We have plenty of help this time. May we call if someone cancels?

☐ We need help supervising a group of children. Please arrive at school by _____.

Thanks for your support.

Field Trip Helpers

Thank you for helping.
Your group of children includes the following:

_____

_____

_____

Keep these children with you at all times. Remind them to use their best behavior.
Other specific instructions:

_____

_____

Sincerely, _____

 ✂ — — — — — — — — — — — — — — — ✂

Field Trip Helpers

Thank you for helping.
Your group of children includes the following:

_____

_____

_____

Keep these children with you at all times. Remind them to use their best behavior.
Other specific instructions:

_____

_____

Sincerely, _____

Thank You!

Dear _____,

Thank you for helping on our field trip!
We couldn't have done it without you!

From all of us in Room _____

✂ - ✂

Thank You!

Dear _____,

Thank you for helping on our field trip!
We couldn't have done it without you!

From all of us in Room _____

6. Behavior Issues

During the school year it may become necessary for you to discuss a child's behavior with his or her parents. Such issues should be dealt with as soon as they arise. The student should be aware of the choices that he or she made and of how these have affected others. Helping the student recognize that he or she has choices is a big step in solving behavior issues. Your goal, for the parents, is to inform them of the situation in question, and to bring them on board in an effort to improve the student's behavior. It is important to share positive as well as negative information with parents. Every parent likes to hear the good things that his or her child does.

Making Better Choices

This form presents a step-by-step process with which students may evaluate possible choices. It gives an opportunity for them to review what happened, what they did, how they felt, and what they might try next time. Students should fill this out with the help of the teacher. (I)

I Always Have a Choice

This visual organizer helps students think about and write down good choices. It can be done independently or with adult supervision. It can be kept on file for the student to review when necessary. (WC)

I'm Proud of Myself

These notes are to be taken home and shared with parents. The messages encourage communication between parents and students regarding good things that occur at school. Students can select notes, or the teacher can pass them out when appropriate. (WC)

Great Behavior

This note is used to celebrate great behavior. When a student does something "great," this is a quick way to celebrate. This note can be filled out by the teacher or by other students, depending on their ages. If a student fills it out, be sure to check and sign it before sending it home. After being sent home for parents to read, these notes can be collected and accumulated for class points or other rewards. (WC)

Good Job!

This letter is a nice way to inform parents of a student's good behavior. When communicating behavior to parents, it is important to share the positive as well as the negative. Use this letter to share good news. (WC)

 # Making Better Choices

My name is _____.

Date: _____

Today I am working on making better choices.

What happened: _____

_____

_____.

What I did: _____

_____

_____.

Why I did it: _____

_____

_____.

How I felt:

☐ Mad   ☐ Frustrated   ☐ Anxious

☐ Lonely   ☐ Confused   ☐ Hurt

Next time I will try to _____

_____

_____.

Signed: _____ Approved: _____

I Always Have a Choice

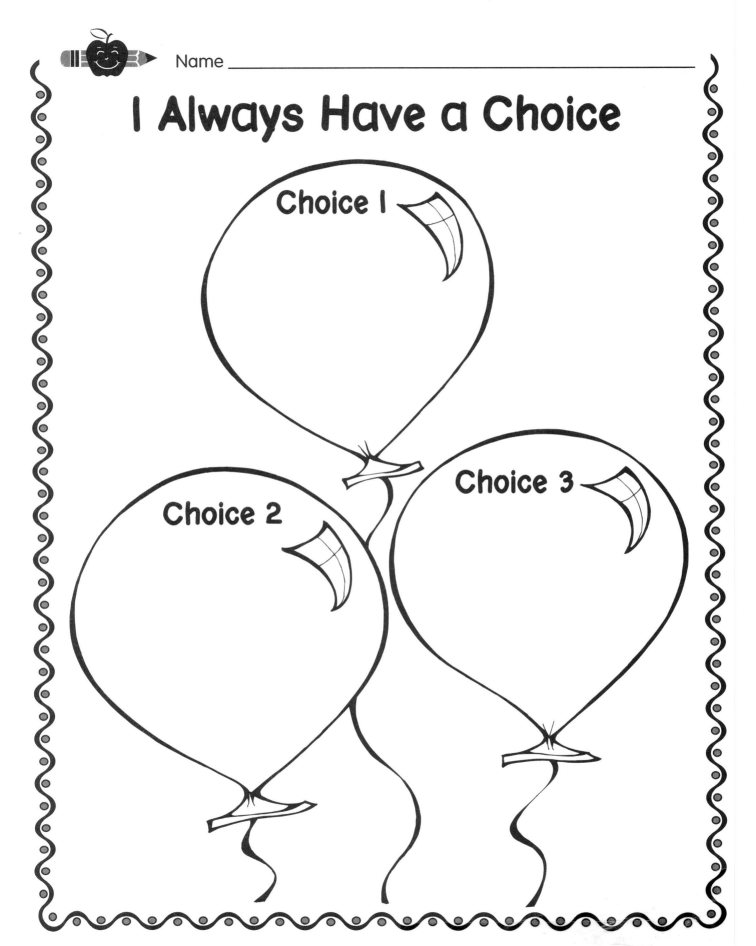

Choice 1

Choice 2

Choice 3

© Fearon Teacher Aids FE111031

I'm Proud of Myself

Dear _____,

Today I did a great job in class. I am proud of myself.
Please ask me what I did!

Love, _____

I'm Proud of Myself

Dear _____,

Today I did a great job in class. I am proud of myself.
Please ask me what I did!

Love, _____

I'm Proud of Myself

Dear _____,

Today I did a great job in class. I am proud of myself.
Please ask me what I did!

Love, _____

GREAT BEHAVIOR

Date: _____

Today _____ did something really great.

She/he _____

_____.

Signed, _____

GREAT BEHAVIOR

Date: _____

Today _____ did something really great.

She/he _____

_____.

Signed, _____

GREAT BEHAVIOR

Date: _____

Today _____ did something really great.

She/he _____

_____.

Signed, _____

© Fearon Teacher Aids FE111031

 # Good Job!

Dear Parent,

I am happy to report that your child, _____ ,

has done a great job on _____ .

She/he has made some great choices. This kind of behavior makes our school a great place.

Signed, _____

 ✂ — ✂

 # Good Job!

Dear Parent,

I am happy to report that your child, _____ ,

has done a great job on _____ .

She/he has made some great choices. This kind of behavior makes our school a great place.

Signed, _____

7. Conferences and Conversations

It is often necessary to discuss an issue with a parent. This may regard a school accomplishment or behavior that needs change. Either way, make all communication with parents as positive as possible. When dealing with a student's inappropriate behavior, focus on the solution rather than belaboring the details of the problem. A note may often be sent home, but sometimes it may be necessary to have the parent come in for a talk.

Note Home

This note informs parents about a choice that their child has made at school. Several options may be checked, letting the parent know what the next step should be. (I)

Parent Update

This note provides an update on school behavior. It may address recurring behavior or a first-time event. Space is provided to detail what has occurred. This allows the parent to get a clear picture of what is going on. There are several options at the bottom of the form that can be selected for follow-up. (I)

Reply to Parent

This form is sent in reply to a parent's expressed concerns. It lets the parent know that you have received his or her call or note and describes the action you have taken. When you receive information or inquiries from parents, your reply is vital. (I)

Good News

This is a note to send home to share some great news. It can be given for a kind act, success in a certain subject, or any action that merits a compliment.

It is important to share good news with parents as well as not-so-good news. (WC)

My Accomplishments

This form tells parents what has been going on in class and gives students an opportunity to write about what they have enjoyed. The form can be filled out by students with your guidance and then taken home to be shared with parents. Make copies if you want to keep these in the students' files or yearly portfolios. (WC)

Stop By or Call Me!

This is a quick, whimsical way to let parents know that you have something fun to tell them. You may have a special success to report or an anecdote about their children. (WC)

Note Home

Date: _____

Dear _____ ,

This note is to keep you informed about _____'s

behavior at school. On _____ ,

the following situation occurred:

_____

_____

_____

_____

_____

_____ .

☐ Please discuss this with your child.

☐ Please let me know what you would like to do about this situation.

☐ Please call; I'd like to hear your ideas about this situation.

☐ Please come in and discuss this with me at your earliest convenience.

☐ Please make an appointment to come in and discuss this.

Thank you.

Signed,

_____

Parent

U P D A T E

Date: _____

Dear _____,

Today at school, _____ made some choices that I would like you to know about.

The incident occurred in/on _____ and involved

_____.

☐ Please discuss this with your child.

☐ Please give me a call at _____.

☐ Please call _____ to make an appointment to come in and

discuss this with _____.

Thank you for your support in this.

Sincerely,

_____

Reply to Parent

Date: _____

Dear _____,

Thanks for asking/telling me about

_____

_____

_____

_____.

☐ I appreciate hearing from you, and this is what I have done: _____

_____.

☐ I have talked to _____ and worked out the problem.

☐ I have set up an appointment with _____ to discuss this issue.

☐ I have discussed this issue with _____ and made plans to

_____.

I am requesting more information from _____.

Please let me know if you have further concerns.

Sincerely,

_____

This note is good news about _____.

Today he/she deserves a great big hug for _____

_____.

Hurray for the good things happening at school!

Sincerely,_____

This note is good news about _____.

Today he/she deserves a great big hug for _____

_____.

Hurray for the good things happening at school!

Sincerely,_____

 Name _____

My Accomplishments

We have been very busy in school.

Date: _____

Dear _____ ,

We have been working on _____
_____
_____ .

I want to tell you about my work on these things: _____
_____
_____
_____
_____
_____
_____ .

I really enjoyed _____

because _____ .

Thanks for letting me share my work with you.

Love,

_____

Stop by or call me.

I want to tell you about

_____

_____

_____

_____

_____ .

Signed, _____

Stop by or call me.

I want to tell you about

_____

_____

_____

_____

_____ .

Signed, _____

8. Self-Esteem

A student who does not have a favorable opinion of his own self worth is at a major disadvantage. It is important for each child to feel like a valuable member of the class. Highlighting each child for a day (or a week) helps him or her experience that sense of importance.

V.I.P. (Very Important Person)

This note lets parents know that their children are being highlighted in the classroom. It should be laminated, attached to a large manila envelope, and sent home so that the student and his or her parents can collect items to be brought in. Send the kit home on the Thursday or Friday before a child's V.I.P. week to allow time for collecting items. (WC)

Person of the Week

This form is to be filled out by the person of the week at school or at home. The completed form is mounted on construction paper and posted in the classroom. It should be displayed for the whole week in a prominent place. When the week is over, the form can be placed in the student's portfolio or added to a class book. (WC)

You're Invited

This note invites the V.I.P.'s parents to visit the classroom. Parents can bring in special treasures and memory items to share with the class. This is a good time for students to share pets, since the animals will have transportation to and from school and adult supervision while at school. Be sure to give parents plenty of advance notice so they can plan their schedules and locate appropriate items to share. If parents are not available, suggest that another relative come in their place. (WC)

It's a Celebration

This letter requests that parents write down a few thoughts about their children that can be read to the class on the children's birthdays or during their V.I.P. weeks. Be sure to send the form home with enough time for parents to fill it out and return it by the special date. (WC)

It's My Birthday

This form highlights a student's uniqueness. The birthday boy or girl can fill it out for his or her special day. It can be filled out either at school or at home. Once filled out, the form can be mounted on construction paper and displayed on the student's birthday.

My Treasure

Most students love to share treasured items with classmates. This form should be filled out and placed with the student's special item on display in the classroom. A picture of the treasure can be drawn in the corner box. (WC)

Dear _____,

Next week we will celebrate your child as our

Very Important Person.

Please place items in this envelope that you would like to have displayed
on the classroom bulletin board.
Include anything that is easy to display but not too precious to leave in the classroom.
These items will be returned to you when the week is over.

Sincerely, _____

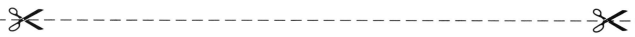

Dear _____,

Next week we will celebrate your child as our

Very Important Person.

Please place items in this envelope that you would like to have displayed
on the classroom bulletin board.
Include anything that is easy to display but not too precious to leave in the classroom.
These items will be returned to you when the week is over.

Sincerely, _____

Person of the Week

Me! _____

I am _____ years old, and I am in the _____ grade.

My Favorites

Food	Color

Animal	Thing to do

My family	Me as a grown-up

For the week of _____ ,

we will be celebrating _____ .

Dear Parents,

We would like you to come to our classroom for a visit. Please bring some special items or memories about _____ to share with us.

Please come on _____ at _____ .

If this is not convenient, please call me at _____ and we'll reschedule.

We are looking forward to your visit.

Thanks,

_____

Dear Parent,

We will be celebrating _____ .

In the space below, please write down a few things about your child for me to share with the class.

Thanks, _____

About _____

by _____

_____

_____

_____

_____

_____

_____ .

It's My Birthday

Today is my special day!
Here's what I have to say!

My full name is _____.

I was born on _____.

My first word was _____.

My favorite toy was _____.

I have _____ brothers and _____ sisters.

I have _____ pets.

My pet's names are _____ and _____.

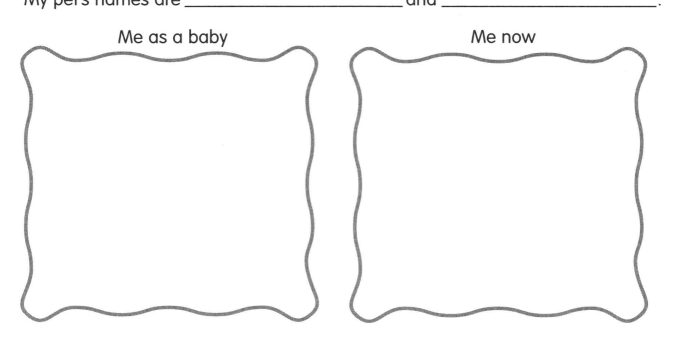

Me as a baby

Me now

© Fearon Teacher Aids FE111031

My Treasure

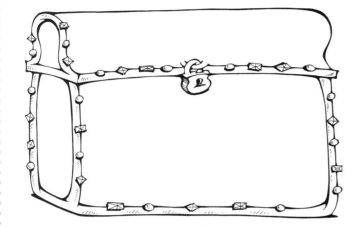

This belongs to

_____ .

It is a

_____ .

It is special because

_____

_____

_____ .

I usually keep it

_____ .

 -

My Treasure

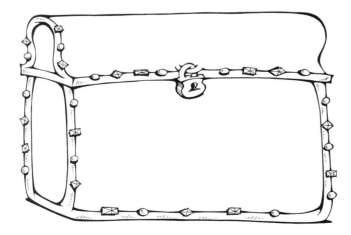

This belongs to

_____ .

It is a

_____ .

It is special because

_____

_____

_____ .

I usually keep it

_____ .

9. End of the Year

As your year comes to an end, there will be many details to take care of. Keeping actively in touch with students' parents is essential to tying up all loose ends and will help your year end as gracefully as it began.

Classroom Cleanup

This note asks parents to look around at home for items that belong at school. Send it out several weeks before the end of the term, early enough for parents to have time to search. If necessary, specific items can be listed for each child. This note can also be used at other times during the year when you do a classroom cleanup. To use during the year, simply delete the words *for the end of the year* before copying. (*WC*)

Grade ____ in Review

This form itemizes subject areas mastered during the year and those needing review. The form helps parents know on which areas their children should work over the summer. (*I*)

Way to Go!

A happy way to send students off to the next grade. These can be given out during a class celebration or slipped into students' folders to be enjoyed at home. The form can be copied onto construction paper for a more festive look. (*WC*)

Read, Read, Read

This reminds parents of the importance of having their children read during summer vacation. Attach a list of recommended books. Parents often feel more comfortable searching out books that have been recommended by the teacher. (*WC*)

Packet of Summer Fun

This note can be attached to work suggested for the summer. Specific skills can be written on the line provided. Using this method, the form can be suited to each child's needs. If individualization is not desired, just write basic topics on the line before copying. (*WC*)

Classroom Cleanup

We're doing a classroom cleanup and we need your help!

Date: _____

Dear Parents,

We are cleaning up our classroom for the end of the year. Please look around your house for anything that might belong to school.

Specific items to look for include:

_____

_____

_____

_____

_____ .

Thanks for your help!

_____

Grade _____ in Review

This year, _____ worked on many concepts. He/she seemed to fully understand the areas of

_____

_____

_____.

Some areas that were difficult for him/her were

_____

_____

_____.

Please review these areas over the summer:

_____

_____

_____.

Feel free to call if you need specific ideas to use in these areas.

Thanks for your support.

Sincerely, _____

First place award for

completing _____ grade!

 Good luck in _____ grade

Signed,

_____

✂ - ✂

First place award for

completing _____ grade!

Good luck in _____ grade

Signed,

_____

Dear Parent,

I hope that you will encourage your child to read this summer. The more you can read to him/her or have your child read to you, the better.

Attached is a list of suggested books. These books are available at the local library or bookstore. Some might be available at used book stores.

Enjoy a summer of good reading.

Packet of Summer Fun

Dear Parent,

Please help your child with these pages during this summer.

By working on _____

each week, your child will be off to a good start for next year.

Enjoy your summer!

Sincerely, _____

- - - ✂ - ✂ - - -

Packet of Summer Fun

Dear Parent,

Please help your child with these pages during this summer.

By working on _____

each week, your child will be off to a good start for next year.

Enjoy your summer!

Sincerely, _____